BORROWED WATER

A Book of American Haiku

BORROWED WATER

WATER

A Book of American Haiku

by the Los Altos Writers Roundtable
Los Altos, California

CHARLES E. TUTTLE CO.: PUBLISHERS
Rutland, Vermont & Tokyo, Japan

Representatives

For Continental Europe:
BOXERBOOKS, INC., *Zurich*

For the British Isles:
PRENTICE-HALL INTERNATIONAL, INC., *London*

For Australasia:
PAUL FLESCH & CO., PTY. LTD., *Melbourne*

*Published by the Charles E. Tuttle Company, Inc.
of Rutland, Vermont and Tokyo, Japan
with editorial offices at
Suido 1-chome, 2–6, Bunkyo-ku, Tokyo*

*Copyright in Japan, 1966
by Charles E. Tuttle Company, Inc.*

*Library of Congress Catalog Card No. 66-26103
First printing, 1966
Second printing, 1967*

Book design by Keiko Chiba
PRINTED IN JAPAN

TO CLEMENT HOYT

TABLE OF CONTENTS

INTRODUCTION

In 1956 the Writers Roundtable of Los Altos, California, was organized by Helen Stiles Chenoweth to further creative writing among adults who were interested in publishing their writings. The poets used the Japanese tone poem haiku to appreciate the syllabic content of words. Use of the haiku taught the prose writers that brevity and simplicity improved their style.

The creating of three rhymeless lines of 5, 7, and 5 syllables, a total of 17, was the first step toward writing poetry. The second was to try the cinquain. Adelaide Crapsey, an American poet who died in 1914, created this from her study of the Japanese *hokku*. (The names *hokku* and haiku are used interchangeably in Japan today but Webster's New International #3 is authority for anglicizing the word haiku.) The cinquain excluded rhyme but included rhythm in the 5 lines, arranged 1, 2, 3, 4, and 1 iambs, in each poem.

The dozen or more poets of the Writers Roundtable who had been studying some of the books mentioned in the bibliography became fascinated with composing their own haiku. They read and discussed the biographies of the four most prominent Japanese poets, Bashō, Buson, Issa, and Shiki, and decided to form a special group devoting all class time to composing American haiku.

In 1963 the *American Haiku* came to the attention of the Group. The founders and editors of this haiku semi-annual were James Bull and Donald Eulert of Platteville, Wisconsin. The editors dedicated their first issue to Harold G. Henderson, author of "Bamboo Broom" and "Introduction to Haiku." Mr. Henderson wrote the editors, "I do believe that one of the greatest functions *American Haiku* could perform is that of being a forum for expression of divergent opinions. . . ."

The dream of the Nippon Gakujutsu Shinkōkai contained in the Special Haiku Report was beginning to come true in Platteville, under the aegis of two enthusiastic men whose dedication to the publishing of haiku was attracting attention all over the United States in their *American Haiku* magazine which was the first to engage in the publication solely of haiku.

A temporary change in editorship brought Mr. Clement Hoyt into the picture and for a year he edited *American Haiku* from his home in Houston, Texas. During this year the haiku Group in Writers Roundtable produced many publishable haiku and became regular contributors to the magazine. Mr. Hoyt sent appreciative letters full of counsel and suggestions which were carefully studied by the Group. In asking for authority on the writing of haiku in English Mr. Hoyt made this statement:

"There is no authority on the haiku in English unless you accept, as I do, the haiku to be a definite form (and to be followed in a like manner) as the sonnet, which was introduced successfully into English from Italian and which has just as definite a restriction of CONTENT as the haiku. Its seventeen syllables, 5, 7, and 5 in three lines, with its restrictions on content, its seasonal implication, its balancing images, its naturalness of expression, its dependence on 'effect' rather than intellectual 'point' is nowhere near as difficult as sonnet's structural and internal restrictions and look how long the sonnet has been part of our literary heritage!"

Nyogen Senzaki, a well-known poet and Mr. Hoyt's teacher, was a perfectionist. He made his pupil write and rewrite haiku for three full years before one was accepted as suitable for publication. Thus Mr. Hoyt passed on for our guidance in the Group's haiku work the necessity for endless rewriting. Three important lessons attained in addition referred to:

1. The beauty and delicacy of Bashō's "let your haiku resemble a willow branch struck by a little shower and trembling a little in the wind."
2. The Japanese masters of haiku produced their best work through observation and meditation.
3. The corollary or contrast, often "far out," which flows from the major thought.

Many of the translators of haiku used rhyme but the Group preferred the 3-line unrhymed English

verse. The Miyamori book used many rhymed translations of well-known writers, a few of whom are:
Basil Hall Chamberlain, Curtis Hidden Page, Lafcadio
Hearn, W. G. Aston, Glenn Shaw, the Japanese trans-
lator Yone Noguchi and the French, Michel Revon.
Although Arthur Waley says, "Japanese poetry can
only be rightly enjoyed in the original", the tradi-
tional and classic form is being very well translated in
English to the public that is growing more and more
haiku-minded.

As Blyth says, "Japanese literature stands or falls
on haiku, but its unique character makes it a difficult
matter to assess its position in world literature." To
the Japanese, poetry is the highest art. In a land with
a language which uses the same word, *sensei*, for poet,
lawyer, and teacher, there are more than a hundred
financially solvent haiku magazines. In the United
States there is but one.

"Borrowed Water" is a group contribution of
haiku composers of Writers Roundtable, Los Altos,
California. It was suggested for publication by Mr.
James Bull, Editor of *American Haiku*, who wrote,
the idea conceived by "the Group has possibilities
which no one else has thought of in this country. You
simply must bring out your book. It will be a valuable
historical record, a beacon guide to others, as well as
a work of art . . . it is essential to the development of
the form (haiku) that it be published."

The book is a selection of some 300 poems, chosen
from more than 700 haiku submitted by the Group in
Writers Roundtable. The haiku have been read,

discussed, criticized and, in some cases, annotated by every member of the Group.

Some of the poems in this book appeared initially in *American Haiku* magazine, which has graciously given their consent for its reproduction here.

Helen Stiles Chenoweth, Editor

Contributors to *Borrowed Water*:

Hilda Aarons	Violet Parks
Margot Bollock	Catherine Neil Paton
Madeline Beattie	Anne Rutherford
Peggy Card	Joy Shieman
Helen S. Chenoweth	Jerri Spinelli
Rosemary Jeffords	Georgian Tashjian
Barbara Ogden Moraw	

SPRING

A small bird's singing
does not announce spring's coming,
but dandelions?

SPRING

Seedlings in the ground
    and snows from the Sierra
        in my sprinkling can.
                —*Tashjian*

My love said good bye
    only this past spring, but—
        what color were his eyes?
                —*Aarons*

Small mud-covered shoes
    tossed behind the kitchen stove.
    Pan whistling in spring.
                —*Rutherford*

Gay kite in the sky
   tugs against tethering string—
      birds boast their freedom.
               —Card

Name faded in stone
   required Braille of fingertips,
      that spring, to free it.
               —Shieman

Baled hay in a neat row,
   still smells wild and sweet:
      my book is finished.
               —Aarons

Near the horizon
  white sails pass—never touching.
    Spring clouds are flying.
                —Jeffords

In an old wooden box
  outside a city window
    yellow daffodils.
                —Rutherford

A leaf flutters down
  to the basket of shade
    you planted years ago.
                —Aarons

Spider-woven trap
   is caught in a web of wind—
      butterflies go free.

              —Jeffords

There he goes again
   pulling threads from cushions.
      Isn't that nest finished?

              —Rutherford

Apple-worm, we see
   even your dark, private world
      has its center star.

              —Shieman

Machines uprooted
 blossoming apricot trees.
  Progress never weeps.
            —Chenoweth

The church bells tolling,
 calling people to worship—
  old man goes fishing.
            —Spinelli

How to say enough,
 so many trees on the hill,
  so many blossoms.
            —Shieman

Early butterfly
   balances on yellow jasmine
      testing new space suit?

>   —Paton

Muddy little hands
   leaving imprints on the heart—
      today the letter.

>   —Beattie

The warm rain falls
   with gentle music. Is it spring
      or a bird that sings?

>   —Jeffords

Tear on a child's cheek—
   even at sorrow's moment
     a rainbow shines there.
            —Shieman

The scent of jasmine
   and the sound of young laughter—
     potpourri of spring.
            —Jeffords

The croaking of frogs
   makes us remember all springs
     that have gone before.
            —Tashjian

Loud the rooster crows,
  Belle nuzzles her new-born calf—
    sweet is the clover.

                    —Spinelli

Strange beam of moonlight
  is locked in agate's cell—
    light in a window.

                    —Chenoweth

Near the letter box
  a nest of infant robins
    all mouth and hunger.

                    —Tashjian

Under the dark earth
  majestic oak is bursting
    its acorn prison.
          —*Rutherford*

Springtime's sudden storm—
  a flash of lightning crackles,
    releasing petals.
          —*Tashjian*

Thrush, in your nest-search
  please use the craggy gray rocks
    of this silent house.
          —*Shieman*

From whence butterflies?
  Thirteen years descends the stairs
  in long yellow gown.

— *Shieman*

A lemon stem
  holds a dozen raindrops—
  a dozen small orchards.

— *Chenoweth*

Leave fallow a small
  corner of this field, son,
    some seeds of thought have wings.

— *Shieman*

. . . *down at heel*
and shaky step, but head held high—
—the scent of lilacs!
—Beattie

Grass muscles through cracks
in the city's stark pavement.
Where have the sheep gone?
—Bollock

Storm of spring creeps up
the beaches' darkened waters;
rainbow in a stone!
—Chenoweth

Gently the butterfly
  rests in a field of clover—
    small hands are quiet.
                    —Spinelli

This lady slipper—
  of course the town cobbler found it—
    the first one of spring.
                    —Tashjian

Carmine-feathered finch
  fighting its own reflection
    feeds orphaned fledglings.
                    —Beattie

Jacaranda bells
　　cannot decide to be roof,
　　　　or lilac-blue rug.
　　　　　　　　—Shieman

Water spirit pleased
　　with spread blossoms—house spirit
　　　　appeased with rice cake.
　　　　　　　　—Moraw

White calla lilies—
　　you can surely tease a croak
　　　　from this plastic frog.
　　　　　　　　—Tashjian

The farmer hears news
    of future crops, the dot-dash
        sound of rain patter.
                —Chenoweth

The moon plays shadows
    on lilacs in full bloom—
        pattern of perfume.
                —Chenoweth

Rain seems soft-fingered,
    but listen to the dewdrop
        land on lemon leaf.
                —Shieman

What sound when a plant
bursts through the soil, what song
if a flower dies?
                    —*Chenoweth*

Apricots blooming—
swirl under fast traffic lanes;
on hair, petalled snow!
                    —*Moraw*

The praying mantis
betrays the twig of the tree.
Late frost blackens buds.
                    —*Chenoweth*

Flowers of paper
  drab and pale at winter's end . . .
    spring brings a crocus.
                    — Bollock

The silent dawn comes
  with hungry gulls' raucous cries
    as the tide steals in.
                    —Chenoweth

A small flower grows
  where decisions met and died
    on top of brave dreams.
                    —Parks

Dewdrops outlining
the new rose leaves, first viewed, show
asymmetrical!
—*Moraw*

Errant white clouds
have settled among black-barked trees
in dogwood time.
—*Tashjian*

Swaying gently
on the tomb of a pharaoh—
a wild poppy flower.
—*Rutherford*

The voices of Spring:
  the turtle, blue jays shrieking,
    hammers on new roofs.
                    —Chenoweth

On the wet, dark street
  cherry blossoms pattern white—
    spring's punctuation.
                    —Card

The snow on the ground
  belies the perfume of petals
    softly drifting down.
                    —Parks

Candle of spring's dawn
lights my darkened window-sill,
sounds of milk cans rise.
— *Chenoweth*

The toes of her shoes
are worn out—wild hyacinths
were lovely this year.
— *Rutherford*

When you hear a sound,
that will be my young seedlings
breaking the black earth.
— *Shieman*

That constant drizzle—
　　a tame wind plays rain-music
　　　on the aspen leaves.
　　　　　　　　—Bollock

If you build your nest,
　　O Robin, in the Star Pine,
　　　bring five friends with you.
　　　　　　　　—Tashjian

Gala flags and bands
　　steady tramp of marching feet—
　　　small dog scans each face.
　　　　　　　　—Beattie

Prayers for white lilac—
no sign of rebirth this spring.
Easter without this?

—Moraw

A small bird's singing
does not announce spring's coming,
but dandelions?

—Chenoweth

SUMMER

The circus parade
  passes by the gaudy zinnias—
    good companions!

Midsummer's coolness
   held in an Owari bowl—
      reeds and pond lilies.
                  —Chenoweth

Summer's hot playtime—
   child's view of weeping cedar—
      hidden toys, secrets!
                  —Moraw

As we ran, our toes
   made dimples in wet sand . . .
      now cups of sea foam.
                  —Parks

Clouds of mosquitoes
      cavorting in summer's dusk—
         curfew of moonlight.

                              —*Chenoweth*

Among the rafters
      of a tulip, a spider
         inspecting his home.

                              —*Bollock*

Strange music of cat
      that woos with caterwauling
         but annoys neighbors.

                              —*Chenoweth*

Tallest of iris
  are the White Cliffs of Dover,
    showing gold dust stored.
                    —Moraw

Sequin-studded sky—
  catch the falling star,
    upend the Big Dipper.
                    —Card

Blowing on a stem
  he laughs as his breath—and dreams—
    reach a far meadow.
                    —Tashjian

In her cottage yard
   hangs a bell, formed of bird seed,
      where her son once played ball.
                              —Aarons

Gently the rain falls,
   each leaf holds its own small notes
      of summer's music.
                              —Chenoweth

Here by the seaside
   sea gulls promenade with me . . .
      footprints tell the tale.
                              —Bollock

Night rides in quickly
    his black steed swaying the grain . . .
        liaison with dawn.
                            —Parks

At early sunrise
    the ancient charred tree trunks glow—
        moment of deceit.
                            —Chenoweth

There in the garden
    the locusts leave their shells
        among the strawflowers.
                            —Tashjian

Dandelion's ghost—
　　in wind-torn gossamer sphere,
　　　spun geometrics!
　　　　　　　　　　—Moraw

A hillside orchard,
　　sweet air scented with apples—
　　　a horse alerted.
　　　　　　　　　　—Spinelli

One night a small boy
　　bathed with the moon in his hands . . .
　　　next day, a rainbow.
　　　　　　　　　　—Chenoweth

Low shadow-leaf cries,
  "Look under me, look under!"
  Lost, mute scarlet ball.
                    —Shieman

On the high meadow
  Tyrian purple weaves
    a heather rug for deer.
                    —Jeffords

Stiff grass near the pond
  in which sky's grey is polished—
    sea gulls come down here.
                    —Aarons

Still no June letter,
   yet arms have rushed to meet it
     on a dozen days.

          —*Shieman*

Dandelion flaunts
   a gold mane on the lawn
    living dangerously.

          —*Paton*

The certain beauty
   of moonlight's cosmetic touch . . .
    no summer wrinkles?

          —*Chenoweth*

Aged men on benches,
   an arcade of trees—
      a jigsaw-puzzle of sky.
                    —Bollock

Curled shadows dancing
   beneath golden shafts of corn—
      flirting winds passing.
                    —Parks

Snail, if you shouted
   in your narrow room, no one
      would hear your great need.
                    —Shieman

The circus parade
  passes by the gaudy zinnias—
    good companions?
                —Chenoweth

Orange Mont Bretia
  breathe flame from an azure vase—
    summer warms her hands.
                —Jeffords

Blue walls and iced tea
  Alice with a green ribbon—
    soon the leaves will turn.
                —Aarons

A lonely gull rides
　　its image in the volute
　　　　even as the waves crash.

　　　　　　　　—Chenoweth

I had forgotten
　　how the fireworks light up
　　　　the idle flowers.

　　　　　　　　—Bollock

He might be watching
　　as I view his cast-off skin—
　　　　two shadow boxers.

　　　　　　　　—Tashjian

Lilies of the water,
    like white gifts on green trays,
      beg to be received.

          —*Shieman*

A crescent moon
    is bent on following the boat
      around the small pond.

          —*Chenoweth*

The jays and squirrels
    co-existing noisily
      in my walnut tree.

          —*Rutherford*

A piccolo breeze
    drops its notes on juniper
        and the scorched brown earth.
                —Aarons

Thumb on garden hose
    spreads spray into water-fan—
        why wait for rainbows?
                —Shieman

All the children
    and picnickers were in wading—
        a small empty bridge!
                —Chenoweth

Summer-heavy leaves
  hang slack and terminal green.
  Autumn . . . let them fly!
          —Bollock

O stuperous snail,
  what night-time frolic took you
  on this tinselled trail?
          —Tashjian

Dripping faces pause
  while meadow larks thrill builders
  with boat-launching theme.
          —Moraw

Lying on the ground
   plumbago blossoms borrow
      blue from sky above.
                    —Chenoweth

The moon shines low
   gleaming on the lotus pool—
      shadows of goldfish tails.
                    —Spinelli

Mite, you are envied
   as you stroll on a petal,
      drowning in purple.
                    —Shieman

The silence of the pool
   is heard above the noise
      of the cataract.

               —Rutherford

The puppy followed
   his water reflection—
      a copycat stranger.

               —Chenoweth

Outside the window
   two humming-birds stand on air—
      emeralds with wings.

               —Jeffords

The leaf fell slowly
 coloring the air yellow
  for just a moment . . .
                    —*Aarons*

Small black-sweatered bee,
 when white blossoms burst at dawn
  you failed to wake me.
                    —*Shieman*

Tin can of daisies,
 on an old scratched table—
  garbage cans below.
                    —*Spinelli*

Slim uptilted moon
   disappears toward morning—
    streets of umbrellas . . .
            —Chenoweth

Home in the hot sand
   the lizards lie, question marks . . .
    countless ones before.
            —Parks

Lilting borrower—
   you took the screen door's hinge-song
    to your high tree top.
            —Tashjian

Fireflies like rockets
  rise from the dark yew trees,
    earth glows an answer.

—Chenoweth

When she went out to pull some beets
  a garter snake lay there sleeping—
    Oh!

—Spinelli

Ice never warmed heart
  so much as when secreted
    from the big ice truck.

—Shieman

Silver tears of rain—
   do you weep for dusty earth
   or for rainbows?
                        —Card

The grass left standing
   by lawnmower's broken blade—
   a killdeer is crying.
                        —Chenoweth

Tonight a balloon
   ripples and floats in the pool—
   no need to fly now . . .
                        —Aarons

Hollowed charred tree stumps
   denied their part of living—
     now bees make honey.
          —Chenoweth

The gulls climb and glide
   on the mounting updraft
     of my admiration.
          —Tashjian

Fern-fingers stretch forth
   green comfort to the wood-lost,
     until he is found.
          —Shieman

One Mind, one seed—
   the certain sky-blue curtain
   of morning glories.
                          —Chenoweth

Fragile green-winged bug
   nestled deep in rose petals—
   do you feel the sun?
                          —Card

At the mountain top
   there are stars to count below
   in the city's night.
                          —Chenoweth

Look! one moonbeam,
   caught below the water's surface,
   has not dulled one bit . . .
          —Aarons

Orchestral summer
   cicada and nightingale—
   will winter be late?
          —Chenoweth

Pssst . . . pssst . . . grasshopper—
   invisible on the reed.
   Yes! I don't see you.
          —Bollock

The constant heart beat
   of my hot desert garden—
     the water meter.

              —Tashjian

Pausing by the weir
   to cull forget-me-nots
     the sky visits me.

              —Chenoweth

Out in the garden
   carrot top niggles defiance—
     gopher—gopher?

              —Spinelli

Listen, a green song,
   melody sweet enough
      to raise buried summer.
                    —*Shieman*

On piled garden cuttings
   a bird is poised, his beak
      higher than corn stalks . . .
                    —*Aarons*

Thick fog on the bay,
   ships tense, fog horns bellowing—
      the next dance is ours.
                    —*Beattie*

Forest fire remnants:
    green blanket of seedling pines
        and black sentinels.

—Chenoweth

One elm leaf slowly
    drops into a basket
        of shade: your eyes are closed.

—Aarons

Little boy bending
    over butterfly's blue wings
        his net forgotten.

—Rutherford

AUTUMN

The thunder rumbles
    but heads of ripened wheat
        are one vast sheet of gold

AUTUMN

Halloween pumpkin
  leering on the window ledge—
    frost's craft held in check.
                    —Bollock

Fawn, dappled statue,
  changed to leaves of flicking brown,
    by some magician.
                    —Shieman

Gold of harvest moon—
  white chrysanthemum in vase
    for the young mother.
                    —Chenoweth

Air filled with autumn,
trees shedding their summer's ware—
are the bears yawning?
                    —Spinelli

Peter Pan's statue
circled by dancing children—
park benches grow cold.
                    —Shieman

An earth mosaic
from the leafy patterns
of late summer rainfall.
                    —Chenoweth

The thunder rumbles
  but heads of ripened wheat
    are one vast sheet of gold.
              —Chenoweth

A deer sniffs the air—
  rustling sound in the bushes,
    is the wind restless?
              —Spinelli

Royalty passed by
  the fields of wheat and barley—
    the scarecrow was silent.
              —Chenoweth

Cold-street memory,
　　buying hot peanuts in shells
　　　from lamp-lit pushcart.
　　　　　　　　　—Shieman

Soldiers march, drums throb—
　　the gentle dove mourns softly
　　　in the pepper tree.
　　　　　　　　　—Paton

Twin pomegranites
　　for my ancient bronze pitcher—
　　　how cross the jays are.
　　　　　　　　　—Paton

Autumn symphony:
  swallows on telegraph wires
    unrehearsed music.

                    —Paton

Red-winged blackbird swings,
  bobbing in the wind, cheers for—
    farmer's roadside weeds!

                    —Moraw

The waning moon swings
  low in the autumn sky,
    to catch a falling star.

                    —Jeffords

That flash of gold flame—
 was it just a wind-swept leaf
  or an oriole?
     —Jeffords

Jack-o-lantern stares
 at the moon-drenched sky. Are they real
  or cloud-witches?
     —Jeffords

Near the sapling oaks
 logs stacked for our winter's fire;
  brittle leaves quiver.
     —Bollock

Voice of the cricket
somewhere near the fireplace—
time to gather logs.
—Chenoweth

A discarded peach stone
grew and produced peaches,
but not the flavor.
—Chenoweth

Sunset in mountains—
parades deep pink and purples,
leaves sorrowing grey.
—Moraw

Yellow goldenrod,
　　purple asters line back road;
　　ghosts pass here barefoot.
　　　　　　　—Moraw

Well-dressed memories
　　recalling thin horse, and man
　　crying, "Rags and bones!"
　　　　　　　—Shieman

. . . the trees are pruned!
　　Now the sunlight can filter
　　down into the roots.
　　　　　　　—Rutherford

Under harvest moon—
  tyger, tyger in the night!
    Marigold eyes stare.
                    —Jeffords

A caterpillar
  must have held a banquet here . . .
    a lacework of leaves.
                    —Bollock

High and away flies
  a departing tribe of birds—
    a time to love and . . . ?
                    —Aarons

Cattails' blunted spears
  offer no resistance
    to invading insects.
                    —Chenoweth

A cricket disturbed
  the sleeping child; on the porch
  a man smoked and smiled.
                    —Chenoweth

Clouds tag the sunlight
  and the season hides itself—
    clothes lines are empty.
                    —Chenoweth

Above city-square
wind claims a partner in tag—
newspaper or dove?
                    —Shieman

Two leaning tombstones
took seventy years to touch—
mist and peace dwell here.
                    —Shieman

South-bound roaring past
splintering the night with sound—
listen! a cricket.
                    —Rutherford

The pure whiteness
   of the chrysanthemums
      defined the smoke-filled room.
               —Chenoweth

The scarecrow is cloaked
   with fog, and fear vanishes—
      blackbirds rest unseen.
               —Chenoweth

The boys are in school;
   fall leaves   the only swimmers
      in the swimming pool.
               —Bollock

A bright harvest moon
shakes a world of tiny mice;
the hunters stir deer.
                    —*Moraw*

Under pampas grass
our white cat, tail curled, gathers dawn
into pink ears.
                    —*Aarons*

The children play
in corn-stalk tepees and watch
the ghost-warriors dance.
                    —*Jeffords*

The church stands lonely . . .
   was it a *Wind Spirit*
      that played the church bells?
                    —*Chenoweth*

Birds on the branches
   like withered leaves, have taken
      sudden wing and flown.
                    —*Parks*

The old gardener
   inhales the crisp air, knowing
      frost will kill the bugs.
                    —*Moraw*

Hounds bay the full moon—
old men breathe hard pursuing
quarry of a dream.

—*Paton*

Geese from gun-metal sea
wedge open the rose dawn,
creating new day.

—*Shieman*

Walking through the dark woods
to the edge of the water—
naked moon bathing!

—*Chenoweth*

Sheep pushing other sheep
    to the top of the hill
        where the grass looks greener.
                    —Rutherford

Twilight comes early;
    sparrow-brown leaves flutter,
        caught by kitten-clawed winds.
                    —Jeffords

The rain-washed roofs—
    radiant geometry
        of moon mathematics.
                    —Chenoweth

Sleep well in your soil
    foreign tree in my garden—
        the sky is the same.

—*Bollock*

The bright harvest moon
    defines pumpkins in the field
        as tangent echoes.

—*Tashjian*

Astringent Autumn
    climbs to a single persimmon
        high on the tree.

—*Chenoweth*

WINTER

Forest fire remnants,
green blanket of seedling pines
and black sentinels.

WINTER

Christmas melts slowly
  in a home filled with children—
    there, love is solid.
            —*Shieman*

The empty hall
  is bleak and lonely; but you'll come
    with coal in your eyes.
            —*Aarons*

In our old oak tree
  the parasitic starlings
    scold the mistletoe.
            —*Tashjian*

The season of rain.
  From eaves onto lemon leaves,
    the staccato drip.

—*Moraw*

Moan of wind in trees . . .
  tongue, court-jester of the mind,
    do not speak of it!

—*Bollock*

To record the feast
  of crumbs we tossed on the snow—
    calligraphy!

—*Tashjian*

Watching moon and stars
with cloud and fog bank rising—
a cold smell of winter.
                —Chenoweth

Thundering feet of waves,
the sea-horses of winter—
sandpipers dance.
                —Chenoweth

Seeing the thin elm
this dismal sunless morning,
I think of yellow.
                —Aarons

Grandma knits a sock,
    grandpa's chair rocks, yet he sleeps;
    snow blocks the roadway.
                        —Spinelli

The old ones pondered
    a pale lemon winter sun
    and bitter fruit.
                        —Card

Hoar frost, hot coffee
    and glint of amber honey—
    did they reach the moon?
                        —Beattie

The scarecrow's clothes hang
  stiff and unimportant at dawn—
    black frost in dress suit?
                    —Chenoweth

The snow lies crisp, cool,
  and white on the hillside.
    Fresh linen for earth's bed?
                    —Jeffords

Winter cloud, grey line
  handwidth from sea-horizon
    captures the sunset!
                    —Shieman

Dark emeralds
   and rubies tossed on white velvet—
     holly in the snow.

               —Jeffords

Cob-webbed wine cellar,
   history of one hundred years—
     let's taste the Gold Rush!

               —Shieman

The tree seems lifeless
   yet the mistletoe prospers—
     a kiss for Christmas?

               —Chenoweth

Somber apartments, flat
   against cold night sky, lit up
     by crossed busy lives.
            —Aarons

Patience tied snow shoes
   but what on earth put these shoes
     on the child's wrong feet?
            —Chenoweth

A wild raging storm
   delighting groundhogs and me—
     no shadows in sight.
            —Tashjian

That eucalyptus
   was lowered to its wet shadow
   by three ant men . . .
                    —*Aarons*

The snow-capped burdock
   nods at the pond ice mirror—
   winter narcissus?
                    —*Jeffords*

Beef soup, toast and milk
   and a forsythia spray
   for your lunch, my love.
                    —*Aarons*

A lonely gull rides
  its image in the volute
    even as the waves crash.
                    —*Chenoweth*

The cold winter wind
  writes its messages in shivers
    on the drifting snow.
                    —*Tashjian*

Hot soup and gold mums
  on the table—dinner time:
    we'll talk our dessert.
                    —*Aarons*

Small birds hovering
　　near dripping eaves of the house—
　　the night cries of snow.
　　　　　　　—Chenoweth

Trying out new leaves
　　the young apricot tree points—
　　which way to heaven?
　　　　　　　—Aarons

Flicker of sunlight
　　on the bed cover—but still
　　a clear shining moon.
　　　　　　　—Chenoweth

On the inland sea
  frozen grass, fringed by the roads,
  stoops old before the sun.
              —*Moraw*

MISCELLANEOUS

Outside the window
    two hummingbirds stand on air—
      emeralds with wings.

MISCELLANEOUS

An old patchwork quilt,
broom and small hands make a tent—
an architect dreams.

—Chenoweth

Scent of cinnamon
and cloves—childhood returns
on crisp ginger-snap wings.

—Jeffords

Kids used to call him
"the old jelly man"
the one with the jack-hammer.

—Bollock

Heirlooms, rocking-horse
sold for a song. Memories dim
the new horizon.

—Paton

The old rug is worn thin—
but would a new one feel
at home in this house?

—Rutherford

Voices of the young
speak from pages turned yellow;
how rich your grey hair!

—Aarons

Drifting into sleep
is the same pillow softer
or the thoughts lighter?
—Rutherford

Shattering silence,
no children's voices—
and a full cooky jar.
—Card

Barracuda gape
caged in the aquarium . . .
a glass horizon.
—Bollock

The pearl of great price
lies always at the bottom.
The ocean is deep.
                    —Rutherford

Hands of time chisel
grotesque and beautiful forms . . .
the shifting desert.
                    —Parks

This monk loves rain
as well as sun and hence does not
mend his umbrella.
                    —Tashjian

Wine comes from the grape—
when drinking, tall not of love.
Love speaks from the heart.
—*Spinelli*

The ship inches out
familiar faces recede—
ending, beginning.
—*Paton*

The old clock ticking
our minutes off day by day—
no one listening.
—*Rutherford*

The same romping wind
   makes a charred wood forest
   and blows out a candle.
                    —Chenoweth

Cob-webbed wine bottles,
   swaddled in time, vintage year
   still corked, untasted.
                    —Shieman

Trapped in a small pot
   with dreams of cool, rippling streams—
   dusty, dry bamboo.
                    —Card

Her niece has gone now;
  she can go back to wearing
    her old purple dress.
            —*Rutherford*

All New England
  in a glass of wild grape jelly
    and a clam bake.
            —Chenoweth

Moon of their first glance
  is moon reflected in tears
    of the last long glance.
            —Shieman

The round, hot, red ball
    has disappeared in the sea—
        night has drowned the day.
                    —*Tashjian*

People stand around
    looking at the fallen tree
        asking who felled it.
                    —*Rutherford*

The butterfly flirts,
    its wings lazy, sips water
        over self image.
                    —*Moraw*

One river flowing
   to the sea, and one rushing—
     but the rhythmic tide . . .
          —Beattie

Between high-rises
   closing in on every side
     one gold-tipped mountain.
          —Rutherford

A game of checkers,
   frowns and determination;
     the soup boiled over . . .
          —Chenoweth

Watching busy ants—
      my clumsy shadow covers
         their entire world.

                              —Bollock

Small fragments of white
      covered the wide desk blotter—
         O wings of failure!

                              —Chenoweth

Water lilies borne,
      like rajahs, down the river . . .
         bridge of destiny.

                              —Parks

My psychology book
   has pressed the pansy's face—
    much more pensive now!
            —Tashjian

The glistening dust
   settles each ant's small movement
    but not the huge trucks!
            —Chenoweth

No bands, no parades,
   the loneliness of silence—
    far away the war.
            —Card

The telephone poles
   prick and puncture the landscape—
      ignoble lodgers?
                  —Bollock

Lightning is flashing,
   thunder calls us from our sleep:
      "You are missing things!"
                  —Bollock

The sea's voice lifting
   defiantly, calling out—
      the same voice answers.
                  —Parks

Sashes, balloons, cake!
  I shall take a ribboned gift—
    and pink aspirin.

                              —Tashjian

Philosophers go!
  Give us more day lilies, more
    crocuses in snow!

                              —Moraw

These Pacific waves—
  touching how many countries
    and the child's feet?

                              —Chenoweth

. . . eyes meeting eyes
  the lace-maker drops a stitch—
    life makes the pattern.

                              —Paton

The pond lies placid;
  night unpacked its darkness there,
    two moons hover here.

                              —Bollock

In the darkened west
  one cloud piped with glowing red—
    joy to a tired tailor.

                              —Tashjian

The book lies open—
　　words are clearly printed
　　　but an unknown tongue.
　　　　　　　—Paton

The slim cat's shadow
　　walks its homeless trail
　　　seeking a new mate.
　　　　　　　—Moraw

Fuji above clouds
　　where mountains should not be found—
　　　and whiter than truth.
　　　　　　　—Aarons

The candle gutters,
no longer gray the drab house—
a saucer of milk.

—Chenoweth

Footsteps echoing
through the city's canyoned walls—
faceless strangers pass.

—Parks

What year, flood so high,
placed round boulder in forked tree—
proof of ghost-waters?

—Moraw

Birds in the garden
explode into chatter—
today lunch was late.

—Card

Clown, slave to laughter,
correctly costumed in coat
of many colors.

—Shieman

The sea is lonely—
vagrant tide has gone shopping
spending sand dollars.

—Chenoweth

O weedless green lawn!
  Oxalis insists on space—
    subversive intent.

> —*Moraw*

The stop signal
  and setting sun's redundancy
    on the red rose garden.

> —*Chenoweth*

Poet sent in space
  describing infinity,
    forgot re-entry.

> —*Shieman*

One leaf a season,
    one bloom a year, one tree, one—
        lifetime study yields!
                        —Moraw

There! a mock ballet . . .
    for someone who likes to look
        at clothes on the line.
                        —Bollock

Were the nuts ripe yet
    or was that a warning rattle
        beneath the tree?
                        —Chenoweth

On mirrored river
    catfish jump through idle dreams—
    No dinner that way.

                        —Moraw

Automobiles swerve
    dodging a plump jaywalker—
    dancing tumbleweed.

                        —Bollock

The old circus clown,
    filling in curves of red smile
        paints dreams and shapes years.

                        —Shieman

Monkey in a tree,
    man on a telegraph pole—
        of human progress.
                    —Chenoweth

It does not appear
    so important today—
        to have shiny floors.
                    —Shieman

Wilderness drama
    when any trail, any turn
        may stir a wild scene.
                    —Moraw

On the great bulldozer
  grey bird balanced and sang—
    below, the freeway.
                        —Card

Small Bonsai tree
  enthroned in Imari bowl
    contemplates the oak.
                        —Card

This land so lavish,
  rich—are we so special then?
  Gold idols smiling.
                        —Beattie

A baby's little fingers
   desperately grasp the milk
     of solace.

               —Parks

Library shelves packed
   with books the boy cannot read—
     his fingers touch them.

               —Paton

From the infinite—
   when the estoppel of thought
     is reached, comes the haiku?

               —Rutherford

BIBLIOGRAPHY

An "Anthology of Haiku, Ancient and Modern" was translated and annotated by Asatarō Miyamori and published in 1932 by Maruzen Company, Ltd., Tokyo, Japan. There are 841 pages of translations, most of them by Miyamori. In this book haiku is a "peculiar form of wit, concentrated to the last degree—the shortest of Japanese poems."

"The Hollow Reed" by Mary J. J. Wrinn was published in 1935 by Harper Bros., New York and London. Eleven pages of haiku information called "In the Japanese Manner" were part of a volume addressed directly to high school and college students. The Wrinn description of haiku is that the poem consists of a "primary statement of thought, out of which grows a secondary thought, corollary to it. This is done in three lines, arranged in five, seven and five syllables."

In 1933 Harold G. Henderson wrote a small book on haiku called "The Bamboo Broom" from which he later wrote "An Introduction to Haiku", an anthology of poems and poets from Bashō to Shiki, which was published by Doubleday & Company, Inc., New York in 1958. Mr. Henderson states ". . . an integral part of Japanese culture . . . the twin arts of reading and writing haiku. Primarily haiku is a poem . . . intended to express and evoke emotion. Haiku may be of many kinds, grave or gay, deep or shallow, religious, satirical, sad, humorous, or charming, but all haiku worthy of the name are records of high moments—higher, at least, than the surrounding plain."

The late R. H. Blyth wrote four books titled "Haiku," published by Hokuseidō in Japan. Vol. I was published in 1949, called "Eastern Culture." Three succeeding volumes, Spring, Summer-Autumn and Autumn-Winter were published up to 1952. In his first volume Blyth wrote, "Haiku is the final flower of Eastern Culture; it is also a way of living. . . . Haiku is haiku, with its own unwritten laws and standards, its aims and achievements. It belongs to a tradition of looking at things, a way of living, a certain tenderness and smallness of mind that avoids the magnificent, the infinite, the eternal. . . . It avoids lyricism and mind coloring both instinctively and consciously."

"Haikai and Haiku" was published in 1958 by the Nippon Gakujutsu Shinkokai in Tokyo. The Japanese Classics Translation Committee in 1934, appointed by the Japanese Society for the Promotion of Science, had for its objective the rendering of Japanese classics into foreign languages as a means of acquainting the world with the cultural and spiritual background of Japan. The first project of the Committee was the translation of the Manyōshū in 1940. The second was the translation of thirty Noh plays, and the third, the work of translating haiku, was commenced in 1946. The Special Haiku Committee stated that the selection of haiku "for translation was based upon:

1) Intrinsic excellence.
2) Cultural and historical value.
3) Appeal to the Western reader. . . .

a source of aesthetic pleasure and diversion, these two elements are skillfully and harmoniously combined in haiku."

Four other books on haiku, in addition to this one, published by Tuttle Company, Tokyo and Rutland, Vermont, are:

"A Net of Fireflies: Japanese Haiku and Haiku Paintings," which includes 33 illustrations in color, contains verse translations and an essay by Harold Stewart. The compilation of haiku on a variety of themes was described by the Hartford *Times* as ". . . . a full year's reading, enjoyably packaged," and by *The Writer's Voice* as a ". . . . metamorphosis into English verse, with spirit, mood, and atmosphere intact."

Ruby Lytle's "What is the Moon: Japanese Haiku Sequence" combines the author's illustrations and haiku, as seen through the eyes of her Siamese kitten. Her poems and white-on-black prints blend beautifully to catch and hold a moment of intuitive insight.

A critical presentation and analysis of Japan's most characteristic literary form is presented by Ken Yasuda in his "The Japanese Haiku: Its Essential Nature,

History, and Possibilities in English, with Selected Examples." The work is a landmark in comparative literature and a standard reference for poets, literature students, poetry lovers, and students of Japanalia.

"Hiroshige's Tokaido in Prints and Poetry" is a beautiful souvenir of Japan embodying two of the greatest achievements of Japanese culture—woodblock prints and poetry. Edited by Reiko Chiba, the book has been lauded as a "charming gift item" with its enchanting makeup, watermarked paper, 55 exquisite full color stamp-sized reproductions and a binding in stenciled fabric.